W9-AUY-353

The
★ ★
UNITED
STATES
PRESIDENTS

William

McKINLEY

Megan M. Gunderson

Big Buddy Books
An Imprint of Abdo Publishing
abdopublishing.com

abdopublishing.com

Published by Abdo Publishing, a division of ABDO, PO Box 398166, Minneapolis, Minnesota 55439.
Copyright © 2017 by Abdo Consulting Group, Inc. International copyrights reserved in all countries. No
part of this book may be reproduced in any form without written permission from the publisher. Big Buddy
Books™ is a trademark and logo of Abdo Publishing.

Printed in the United States of America, North Mankato, Minnesota
062016
092016

 THIS BOOK CONTAINS
RECYCLED MATERIALS

Design: Sarah DeYoung, Mighty Media, Inc.
Production: Mighty Media, Inc.
Editor: Liz Salzmann
Cover Photograph: Getty Images
Interior Photographs: American Political History (p. 19); AP Images (pp. 7, 29); Corbis (pp. 7, 17, 23, 27);
    Library of Congress (pp. 5, 6, 13, 15, 21); National Archives (p. 25); Picture History (pp. 9, 11)

Cataloging-in-Publication Data

Names: Gunderson, Megan M., author.
Title: William McKinley / by Megan M. Gunderson.
Description: Minneapolis, MN : Abdo Publishing, [2017] | Series: United States
    presidents | Includes bibliographical references and index.
Identifiers: LCCN 2015957553 | ISBN 9781680781083 (lib. bdg.) |
    ISBN 9781680775280 (ebook)
Subjects: LCSH: McKinley, William, 1843-1901--Juvenile literature. |
    Presidents--United States--Biography--Juvenile literature. | United States--
    Politics and government--1897-1901--Juvenile literature.
Classification: DDC 973.8/8092 [B]--dc23
LC record available at http://lccn.loc.gov/2015957553

Contents

William McKinley

William McKinley was the twenty-fifth president of the United States. He was a leading member of the **Republican** Party. First, he was elected to the US House of **Representatives**. Later, he became governor of Ohio.

After he was elected president, he led the country through the **Spanish-American War**. The nation gained new territories. Americans also continued to be financially successful. McKinley was reelected in 1900. But he was **assassinated** soon after his second term began.

Timeline

1843

On January 29, William McKinley was born in Niles, Ohio.

1871

McKinley married Ida Saxton on January 25.

1862

McKinley took part in the Battle of Antietam during the **American Civil War**.

1876

McKinley was elected to the US House of **Representatives**.

1896

McKinley was elected the twenty-fifth US president.

1898

The United States fought and won the **Spanish-American War**.

1891

McKinley was elected governor of Ohio.

1901

On September 6, Leon F. Czolgosz shot McKinley. On September 14, William McKinley died.

Ohio Youth

William McKinley was born in Niles, Ohio, on January 29, 1843. When William was nine, his family moved to Poland, Ohio. There, William attended school.

Later, William attended college in Pennsylvania. After college, William became a teacher.

★ FAST FACTS ★

Born: January 29, 1843

Wife: Ida Saxton (1847–1907)

Children: two

Political Party: Republican

Age at Inauguration: 54

Years Served: 1897–1901

Vice Presidents: Garret A. Hobart, Theodore Roosevelt

Died: September 14, 1901, age 58

William's parents, William
and Nancy Allison McKinley

Civil War Hero

The **American Civil War** began in April 1861. In June, McKinley joined the **Union** army. In September 1862, McKinley was at the Battle of Antietam. McKinley was in charge of the food supplies. He braved enemy fire to bring his fellow soldiers food during the battle.

After the war, McKinley studied law. In 1867, he became a **lawyer**. He opened an office in Canton, Ohio. McKinley did well as a lawyer. He soon joined George W. Belden's law practice.

McKinley survived one of the deadliest single-day battles of the Civil War. More than 20,000 soldiers died in the Battle of Antietam.

Law and Family

In 1869, McKinley was elected **prosecuting attorney** of Stark County, Ohio. He often spoke out for unpopular causes.

Around this time, McKinley met Ida Saxton. McKinley and Ida married on January 25, 1871. They had two daughters. Sadly, both girls died as young children.

McKinley continued his work. But his wife was unhappy. She became sickly and never got completely well. McKinley did his best to help and comfort her throughout his life.

Ida Saxton was the daughter of a banker. She worked in her father's bank before she married McKinley.

13

Congressman

In 1876, McKinley was elected to the US House of **Representatives**. In 1883, McKinley voted for the Pendleton **Civil Service** Act.

Before this, people were given civil service jobs based on their **political** party. The new act required people to pass tests to get these jobs.

McKinley also **supported** an act that helped **veterans** of the **American Civil War**. The act provided money to veterans if they ever became disabled.

Ohio senator
George H. Pendleton
wrote the Pendleton
Civil Service Act.

In Congress, McKinley worked to improve the nation's **economy**. But many people didn't like some of the laws he voted for. Partly because of this, McKinley was not reelected in 1890.

Although he lost the congressional election, McKinley was still a popular **politician**. So, the **Republicans** chose him to run for governor of Ohio in 1891. McKinley easily won the election. He served two terms.

Governor McKinley improved the state's waterways and roads. He also continued to help the economy.

★ DID YOU KNOW? ★

McKinley always wore a red **carnation** in the buttonhole of his coat.

While McKinley was governor, he continued to support the Republican Party. He made hundreds of speeches for Republican candidates for Congress in 1894.

Election of 1896

McKinley was popular in the **Republican** Party. At the 1896 **Republican National Convention**, he was chosen to run for president. McKinley ran against **Democrat** William Jennings Bryan of Nebraska.

McKinley and Bryan campaigned differently. Bryan went around the country making speeches and meeting voters. McKinley stayed home. From there, he greeted the thousands of people who came to Canton. This became known as the "front porch campaign."

McKinley made campaign speeches from his home in Canton, Ohio.

America's money system was a big campaign subject. McKinley was for the gold standard. This meant that paper money could be traded in for a specific amount of gold. Bryan backed the free silver system. This would allow an unlimited number of silver coins to be made.

McKinley easily won the election. The same year, the **Republican** Party gained control of the Senate and the House. The party would remain in power for the next 14 years.

★ DID YOU KNOW? ★

McKinley signed the Gold Standard Act into law with a special gold pen.

Garret A. Hobart was vice president during McKinley's first term.

President

President McKinley took office in 1897. On February 15, 1898, the battleship USS *Maine* exploded and sank. Most people believed Spain had blown up the ship. President McKinley ordered an **investigation**. The report stated that the ship had been blown up on purpose.

On April 25, 1898, the United States started a war with Spain. This was the **Spanish-American War**. The United States quickly won the war. The two countries then signed the **Treaty** of Paris on December 10.

PRESIDENT McKINLEY'S CABINET

First Term
March 4, 1897–March 4, 1901

★ **STATE:** John Sherman,
William R. Day (from April 28, 1898),
John Hay (from September 30, 1898)

★ **TREASURY:** Lyman J. Gage

★ **WAR:** Russell A. Alger,
Elihu Root (from August 1, 1899)

★ **NAVY:** John D. Long

★ **ATTORNEY GENERAL:** Joseph McKenna,
John W. Griggs (from February 1, 1898)

★ **INTERIOR:** Cornelius N. Bliss,
Ethan A. Hitchcock (from February 20, 1899)

★ **AGRICULTURE:** James Wilson

Second Term
March 4, 1901–September 14, 1901

★ **STATE:** John Hay

★ **TREASURY:** Lyman J. Gage

★ **WAR:** Elihu Root

★ **NAVY:** John D. Long

★ **ATTORNEY GENERAL:** John W. Griggs,
Philander C. Knox (from April 10, 1901)

★ **INTERIOR:** Ethan A. Hitchcock

★ **AGRICULTURE:** James Wilson

The **Treaty** of Paris freed Cuba from Spanish control. It also gave the United States more territory. The nation gained Puerto Rico, Guam, and the Philippines.

While McKinley was in office, the United States also claimed other territories. This included the Hawaiian Islands and Wake Island in the Pacific Ocean. In 1899, the United States got some of the Samoa Islands. Germany controlled the rest of them.

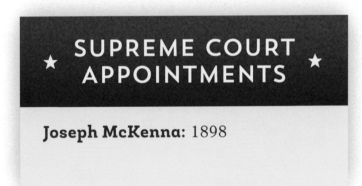

SUPREME COURT APPOINTMENTS

Joseph McKenna: 1898

Congress started working to gain the Hawaiian Islands in 1897. Hawaii became a US territory in 1900.

H. Res. 259.

Public Resolution no 57

Fifty-fifth Congress of the United States of America;

At the Second Session,

Begun and held at the City of Washington on Monday, the sixth day of December, one thousand eight hundred and ninety-seven.

JOINT RESOLUTION

To provide for annexing the Hawaiian Islands to the United States.

Whereas the Government of the Republic of Hawaii having, in due form, signified its consent, in the manner provided by its constitution, to cede absolutely and without reserve to the United States of America all rights of sovereignty of whatsoever kind in and over the Hawaiian Islands and their dependencies, and also to cede and transfer to the United States the absolute fee and ownership of all public, Government, or Crown lands, public buildings or edifices, ports, harbors, military equipment, and all other public property of every kind and description belonging to the Government of the Hawaiian Islands, together with every right and appurtenance thereunto appertaining: Therefore,

Resolved by the Senate and House of Representatives of the United States of America in Congress assembled, That said cession is accepted, ratified, and confirmed, and that the said Hawaiian Islands and their dependencies be, and they are hereby, annexed as a part of the territory of the United States and are subject to the sovereign dominion thereof, and that all and singular the property and rights hereinbefore mentioned are vested in the United States of America.

The existing laws of the United States relative to public lands shall not apply to such lands in the Hawaiian Islands; but the Congress of the United States shall enact special laws for their management and disposition : *Provided,* That all revenue from or proceeds of the same, except as regards such part thereof as may be used or occupied for the civil, military, or naval purposes of the United States, or may be assigned for the use of the local government, shall be used solely for the benefit of the inhabitants of the Hawaiian Islands for

A Tragic Ending

In 1900, President McKinley ran for reelection. Vice President Hobart had died in office the year before. New York governor Theodore Roosevelt ran as McKinley's vice president.

Once again, McKinley ran against William Jennings Bryan. And again, McKinley easily won the election. President McKinley then began a trip through the western states. At the end of the tour, McKinley went to the Pan-American **Exposition** in Buffalo, New York.

On September 5, 1901, President McKinley spoke at the Pan-American Exposition. More than 50,000 people listened to his speech!

On September 6, 1901, President McKinley attended an event at the Pan-American **Exposition**. Hundreds of people there waited to shake his hand.

Leon F. Czolgosz was among the guests. Czolgosz held a gun hidden under a **handkerchief**. When President McKinley reached to shake his hand, Czolgosz shot him twice.

William McKinley died on September 14, 1901. He holds an important place in US history for the territories gained during his presidency.

★ DID YOU KNOW? ★

McKinley's last words were, "Good-bye, all. It is God's way. His will, not ours be done."

Leon F. Czolgosz
was found guilty of
McKinley's murder.

Office of the President

Branches of Government

The US government has three branches. They are the executive, legislative, and judicial branches. Each branch has some power over the others. This is called a system of checks and balances.

★ Executive Branch

The executive branch enforces laws. It is made up of the president, the vice president, and the president's cabinet. The president represents the United States around the world. He or she also signs bills into law and leads the military.

★ Legislative Branch

The legislative branch makes laws, maintains the military, and regulates trade. It also has the power to declare war. This branch includes the Senate and the House of Representatives. Together, these two houses form Congress.

★ Judicial Branch

The judicial branch interprets laws. It is made up of district courts, courts of appeals, and the Supreme Court. District courts try cases. Sometimes people disagree with a trial's outcome. Then he or she may appeal. If a court of appeals supports the ruling, a person may appeal to the Supreme Court.

Qualifications for Office

To be president, a candidate must be at least 35 years old. The person must be a natural-born US citizen. He or she must also have lived in the United States for at least 14 years.

Electoral College

The US presidential election is an indirect election. Voters from each state choose electors. These electors represent their state in the Electoral College. Each elector has one electoral vote. Electors cast their vote for the candidate with the highest number of votes from people in their state. A candidate must receive the majority of Electoral College votes to win.

Term of Office

Each president may be elected to two four-year terms. The presidential election is held on the Tuesday after the first Monday in November. The president is sworn in on January 20 of the following year. At that time, he or she takes the oath of office.
It states:

I do solemnly swear (or affirm) that I will faithfully execute the office of President of the United States, and will to the best of my ability, preserve, protect and defend the Constitution of the United States.

Line of Succession

The Presidential Succession Act of 1947 states who becomes president if the president cannot serve. The vice president is first in the line. Next are the Speaker of the House and the President Pro Tempore of the Senate. It may happen that none of these individuals is able to serve. Then the office falls to the president's cabinet members. They would take office in the order in which each department was created:

Secretary of State

Secretary of the Treasury

Secretary of Defense

Attorney General

Secretary of the Interior

Secretary of Agriculture

Secretary of Commerce

Secretary of Labor

Secretary of Health and Human Services

Secretary of Housing and Urban Development

Secretary of Transportation

Secretary of Energy

Secretary of Education

Secretary of Veterans Affairs

Secretary of Homeland Security

Benefits

★ While in office, the president receives a salary. It is $400,000 per year. He or she lives in the White House. The president also has 24-hour Secret Service protection.

★ The president may travel on a Boeing 747 jet. This special jet is called Air Force One. It can hold 70 passengers. It has kitchens, a dining room, sleeping areas, and more. Air Force One can fly halfway around the world before needing to refuel. It can even refuel in flight!

★ When the president travels by car, he or she uses Cadillac One. It is a Cadillac Deville that has been modified. The car has heavy armor and communications systems. The president may even take Cadillac One along when visiting other countries.

★ The president also travels on a helicopter. It is called Marine One. It may also be taken along when the president visits other countries.

★ Sometimes the president needs to get away with family and friends. Camp David is the official presidential retreat. It is located in Maryland. The US Navy maintains the retreat. The US Marine Corps keeps it secure. The camp offers swimming, tennis, golf, and hiking.

★ When the president leaves office, he or she receives lifetime Secret Service protection. He or she also receives a yearly pension of $203,700. The former president also receives money for office space, supplies, and staff.

PRESIDENTS AND THEIR TERMS

PRESIDENT	PARTY	TOOK OFFICE	LEFT OFFICE	TERMS SERVED	VICE PRESIDENT
George Washington	None	April 30, 1789	March 4, 1797	Two	John Adams
John Adams	Federalist	March 4, 1797	March 4, 1801	One	Thomas Jefferson
Thomas Jefferson	Democratic-Republican	March 4, 1801	March 4, 1809	Two	Aaron Burr, George Clinton
James Madison	Democratic-Republican	March 4, 1809	March 4, 1817	Two	George Clinton, Elbridge Gerry
James Monroe	Democratic-Republican	March 4, 1817	March 4, 1825	Two	Daniel D. Tompkins
John Quincy Adams	Democratic-Republican	March 4, 1825	March 4, 1829	One	John C. Calhoun
Andrew Jackson	Democrat	March 4, 1829	March 4, 1837	Two	John C. Calhoun, Martin Van Buren
Martin Van Buren	Democrat	March 4, 1837	March 4, 1841	One	Richard M. Johnson
William H. Harrison	Whig	March 4, 1841	April 4, 1841	Died During First Term	John Tyler
John Tyler	Whig	April 6, 1841	March 4, 1845	Completed Harrison's Term	Office Vacant
James K. Polk	Democrat	March 4, 1845	March 4, 1849	One	George M. Dallas
Zachary Taylor	Whig	March 5, 1849	July 9, 1850	Died During First Term	Millard Fillmore

PRESIDENT	PARTY	TOOK OFFICE	LEFT OFFICE	TERMS SERVED	VICE PRESIDENT
Millard Fillmore	Whig	July 10, 1850	March 4, 1853	Completed Taylor's Term	Office Vacant
Franklin Pierce	Democrat	March 4, 1853	March 4, 1857	One	William R.D. King
James Buchanan	Democrat	March 4, 1857	March 4, 1861	One	John C. Breckinridge
Abraham Lincoln	Republican	March 4, 1861	April 15, 1865	Served One Term, Died During Second Term	Hannibal Hamlin, Andrew Johnson
Andrew Johnson	Democrat	April 15, 1865	March 4, 1869	Completed Lincoln's Second Term	Office Vacant
Ulysses S. Grant	Republican	March 4, 1869	March 4, 1877	Two	Schuyler Colfax, Henry Wilson
Rutherford B. Hayes	Republican	March 3, 1877	March 4, 1881	One	William A. Wheeler
James A. Garfield	Republican	March 4, 1881	September 19, 1881	Died During First Term	Chester Arthur
Chester Arthur	Republican	September 20, 1881	March 4, 1885	Completed Garfield's Term	Office Vacant
Grover Cleveland	Democrat	March 4, 1885	March 4, 1889	One	Thomas A. Hendricks
Benjamin Harrison	Republican	March 4, 1889	March 4, 1893	One	Levi P. Morton
Grover Cleveland	Democrat	March 4, 1893	March 4, 1897	One	Adlai E. Stevenson
William McKinley	Republican	March 4, 1897	September 14, 1901	Served One Term, Died During Second Term	Garret A. Hobart, Theodore Roosevelt

PRESIDENT	PARTY	TOOK OFFICE	LEFT OFFICE	TERMS SERVED	VICE PRESIDENT
Theodore Roosevelt	Republican	September 14, 1901	March 4, 1909	Completed McKinley's Second Term, Served One Term	Office Vacant, Charles Fairbanks
William Taft	Republican	March 4, 1909	March 4, 1913	One	James S. Sherman
Woodrow Wilson	Democrat	March 4, 1913	March 4, 1921	Two	Thomas R. Marshall
Warren G. Harding	Republican	March 4, 1921	August 2, 1923	Died During First Term	Calvin Coolidge
Calvin Coolidge	Republican	August 3, 1923	March 4, 1929	Completed Harding's Term, Served One Term	Office Vacant, Charles Dawes
Herbert Hoover	Republican	March 4, 1929	March 4, 1933	One	Charles Curtis
Franklin D. Roosevelt	Democrat	March 4, 1933	April 12, 1945	Served Three Terms, Died During Fourth Term	John Nance Garner, Henry A. Wallace, Harry S. Truman
Harry S. Truman	Democrat	April 12, 1945	January 20, 1953	Completed Roosevelt's Fourth Term, Served One Term	Office Vacant, Alben Barkley
Dwight D. Eisenhower	Republican	January 20, 1953	January 20, 1961	Two	Richard Nixon
John F. Kennedy	Democrat	January 20, 1961	November 22, 1963	Died During First Term	Lyndon B. Johnson
Lyndon B. Johnson	Democrat	November 22, 1963	January 20, 1969	Completed Kennedy's Term, Served One Term	Office Vacant, Hubert H. Humphrey
Richard Nixon	Republican	January 20, 1969	August 9, 1974	Completed First Term, Resigned During Second Term	Spiro T. Agnew, Gerald Ford

PRESIDENT	PARTY	TOOK OFFICE	LEFT OFFICE	TERMS SERVED	VICE PRESIDENT
Gerald Ford	Republican	August 9, 1974	January 20, 1977	Completed Nixon's Second Term	Nelson A. Rockefeller
Jimmy Carter	Democrat	January 20, 1977	January 20, 1981	One	Walter Mondale
Ronald Reagan	Republican	January 20, 1981	January 20, 1989	Two	George H.W. Bush
George H.W. Bush	Republican	January 20, 1989	January 20, 1993	One	Dan Quayle
Bill Clinton	Democrat	January 20, 1993	January 20, 2001	Two	Al Gore
George W. Bush	Republican	January 20, 2001	January 20, 2009	Two	Dick Cheney
Barack Obama	Democrat	January 20, 2009	January 20, 2017	Two	Joe Biden

"Equality of rights must prevail, and our laws be always and everywhere respected and obeyed." William McKinley

★ WRITE TO THE PRESIDENT ★

You may write to the president at:
The White House
1600 Pennsylvania Avenue NW
Washington, DC 20500

You may e-mail the president at:
comments@whitehouse.gov

37

Glossary

American Civil War—the war between the Northern and Southern states from 1861 to 1865.

assassinate—to murder an important person by a surprise or secret attack.

carnation—a pink, white, yellow, or red flower that has a sweet smell.

civil service—the part of the government that is responsible for matters not covered by the military, the courts, or the law.

Democrat—a member of the Democratic political party.

economy—the way that a country produces, sells, and buys goods and services.

exposition—a large event where new inventions or products are displayed.

handkerchief—a small cloth used for wiping the face, nose, or eyes.

investigation—the act of gathering information about or studying something.

lawyer (LAW-yuhr)—a person who gives people advice on laws or represents them in court.

politics—the art or science of government. Something referring to politics is political. A person who is active in politics is a politician.

prosecuting attorney—a lawyer who represents the government in court cases.

representative—someone chosen in an election to act or speak for the people who voted for him or her.

Republican—a member of the Republican political party.

Republican National Convention—a meeting during which the Republican Party chooses candidates for president and vice president.

Spanish-American War—a war fought between the United States and Spain in 1898.

support—to believe in or be in favor of something.

treaty—an agreement made between two or more groups.

Union—the Northern states that remained part of the United States during the American Civil War.

veteran—a person who has served in the armed forces.

★ WEBSITES ★

To learn more about the US Presidents, visit **booklinks.abdopublishing.com**. These links are routinely monitored and updated to provide the most current information available.

Index